Florilegium

Florilegium

Florilegium

Florilegium, an audio representation of selected pieces from this book is available for purchase. The full collection of albums is available via the website below and all good streaming sites and music retailers.

Merchandise and contact: www.theorator.bigcartel.com

Mailing list sign up: www.eepurl.com/ciAZBD

Social media:
Twitter: @TheOrator_UK
Instagram: @TheOrator_UK

Best place to catch a live show?
Anywhere. Everywhere. Otherwise, see above.

Florilegium

Manifesto.
of
Artist integrity.

First we reject all schisms and isms.
We exist beyond temporary definition.
The academies and institutions that have for so long held art their captive shall be permitted to keep their rank, insofar it is overstood that any metrics provided by academies and institutions of all ilk shall be their concern. Today and for all days, historic and established traditional rank of art is rendered opinion. The artist's integrity will be absolute and the final measure of a body of work.
Change is essential to the growth of life. As such we embrace tides of change. The time is always now. Art is a way of life. The cost of life is the release of inhibitions, and the normal. The artist is an embodiment of life. He/she is expected to reflect that existence, meanwhile constantly, challenging that existence by the exploration of the other side. Be not afraid of the other side.
The artist should embrace critique like the thorny friend that sticks by your side. The artist has no enemies. Critique is opinion. How heavy is a glass of water? Exactly. The artist must be the first critic. The artist must be the worst critic. Your art is your unwavering word, you will live by it as normal, you will die by it if the call is so. Defend art, venomously. Defend integrity, aggressively. The artist is the centre of their universe. The artist wears responsibility like suits of valor. The Poet is the primary defender of the people. The Painter is the primary historian. The responsibility of art preservation belongs to all. Art and culture are inseparable. Culture is the primary carrier of art. Defend culture, venomously. There is no better representation than the real thing. If it is not the real thing, it is not art. Representations of art are fine insofar they are acknowledged as so. There is a thin difference between art and representation of art. The line exists. Acknowledge it. The artist must be a victim of his or her own greatness, or laziness.

Either way, the artist must know they exist. Doubt does not exist on the plane we exist on. You are great. This does not mean you are there. Keep working. Until the worlds problems are solved, the artist's duty remains intact and whole. The recognition of ones internal power to create is in fact marginal compared to the full extent of your ability. Excellence is not a bar but a line. Draw this line. Embrace critique. Critique is opinion. How heavy is a glass of water? Exactly. Rules are for those who accept them. Rules at best are creative tools. Reject mediocrity, question power. Artists walk amongst men. Politics and art are inseparable. We accept this to be a self-evident truth. The use of art solely as a means of entertainment is rejected. Art for art's sake is shit, the colour of the sky need not be the topic of any poem from hereon in. Qualifications are the bane of the creative. Art is best cured in travel and dispensed with passion. The earth is important to life on earth, as such the earth is important to art. Life without art is unimaginable, we run dangerously fast in the direction of life carried on the wings of art, spreading its news as we go. Art is catharsis. Expression allows the artist to remain functionally insane. The artist must express. The artist will indefinitely pursue balance.

Balance is best achieved in motion.

Forward artists of the universe, forward.

Florilegium

Florilegium
CONTENTS

CONTENTS I

Journey 12
Black 13
I Saw The Hustle Die 14
No Contribution 16
My Drum 18
Time Is Not Promised 20
Forward 22
Tek Time 23
.45 25
Seek 27
Poetry Will Be Free 30
Twenty Six 32
PEACE 34
Tertiary 35
Ruckus 36
P.S Don't @ Me 37
The Prettiest Nitty 39
Special Brew 40
Call The Cartographer 42
Breathe 43
History 44
City Lights 46
Firm Ground 47
Carrie 48
N I G G A 49
My Son 50
UoB Intertextuality 51
How Are You Today? 52
Dawn 53
Clap 54
A 3AM Walk 55
H N I C 56
No Social Class 58
Do You Know Your Wrongs? 59

CONTENTS II

Ruby Red Day 60
Uhmm Hmm 62
HATE 63
Mobilise 64
The Every Day Struggle 67
Wool 68
17 Slaves 69
WAR 71
The Dojo 72
Rubin Carter 75
Gallows 77
Don't Turn Your Back 78
Raised Up 80
Woop Woop! Wake Up 81
Do What It Do 82
Say Something 83
Butterflies 84
Money Hold Who? 86
I Will 87
My Friend 89
Who? 91
Wandering Child Of Maroon Town 94
Candy Man 96
Bandulu 98
Alpaca Rug 99
Sunken Place 100
Herb Seeker 101
The 0116 102
New Home 104
Banana Juice 105
Constant 106
Teary Estuary 107
A Beauty Lost 108
I Too Shall Miss You 109
Word Power 110

Journey

Journey after journey
Each step by step
All in the name of progress
Journey by journey
Step after step
All in the name of progress
Nay has a man ever travelled to find himself
They travel to find the qualities of self lacking in possession
No man has ever found himself in transit
But frequently do they find things to cause the exponential growth of self
The kind of things that can be heard mumbled high above the wishing well
No soul can kiss and tell
If you wasn't there you couldn't know
We all have a truth
More time you have to write your own
Prescription truth is placebo
What could there ever be to reap
If you are yet to sow?
So, I encourage you to get up and go
Journey after journey
Each step by step
All in the name of progress
Journey by journey
Step after step
All in the name of progress

Black

Draw your swords comrades for now is the time to go to war

Ensure your ink is brimming

Nib nestled and ready

For now tis the time to wreak havoc on the naysayers, nay doers

Pessimists in the social penthouses

And the cynics in the sewers

Fuck 'em all

We ouchea

My sword knows no race colour or creed

In black I bleed

D'Fuck does my sword care for punkish responses spewed by tongues

In response to ones truth?

My sword has no tongue to hold

Its loooose…

Like May's grip on the future after June

Before this there was a caution

A tiptoeing around the page

Now, rage and contortion

In the scrawling of my debilities disguised as dogmatic soliloquies

Release yourself from what you think you heard

My sword calls falsehood on your idols

Try me

My pen is my sword and it is mightier than the mouse

Exposing gashes in the manhood of any idol heavy with click laden clout

Meet me in the real world

Impress me with your motherfucking mind

Although, in truth

You don't have to do a motherfucking thing

Like I've got no business stopping this sword swing

Don't play with my pen

It knows no race, colour or creed

Has no filter

And black is the colour it bleeds

I Saw The Hustle Die

I saw the hustle die G
Things aren't the same no mo'
There ain't no money in the streets like there used to be
You'd be hard pressed leaving your house in the AM to make an earner
Enough for a burger in PM
Blue murder for the blue collar worker
But we're all in it together says the PM

Yet there ain't no money in the streets like there used to be
Wheelers and dealers are things of nostalgia
Tea leaves are half as active, doing half a job
Charging over the odds, when you want the lot
Talking of lots, there's not much money in motors
It's a full days job spinning a bacon sarnie out of a few 95 rovers

Shit ain't the same no mo'
There ain't no money and there ain't no honey
Funny where and funny how?
My generation be like 'Preach brudda man preach!'
But them fifties and sixties babies neatly grasp what I'm on about

Fuck it, all this money in England is clearly disguised
I have the truth my friends, I tell no lies
The Tories stumbled upon a money tree once upon a time
They built the most beautiful garden - to protect it from outside
And said 'the tree is yours people, though we will provide'
And when the fruit was plump and the trunk strong
The whole bloody garden was privatized

So there ain't no money in the streets like there used to be
I saw the hustle die G
It's the year 2019
Hustlers of street savvy have become entrepreneurs
Free from the mundane
Though they are still trapping you
And they are still trapping yours
So we are still trapping flavours
Politicians still yapping jaws
Still coked up
Still over taxing the poor
Still selling hope to a nation struggling to stand anymore

I saw the hustle die B
But I am told I never seen what I saw

I saw the hustle die B
And shit just ain't the same no mo'

No Contribution

Make no contribution to the fuckery
Let it be your solemn duty to uphold and preserve the real
Make no contribution to the fuckery
Let it be your solemn duty to uphold and preserve the real
Be at the jugular of any who mislead, misrepresent or mistake the real for anything other
than what it motherfucking is
FREE the REAL
FREE the MOTHERFUCKING REAL
Any attempt to dislodge representatives of the real will be met with force
Fuck your discourse, this be a new narrative
Containing no carrot stick for the ignorant or consciously poor
Lay waste to how it was, embrace how it will be from henceforth
Claims of wealth, or manhood
Will be required to provide evidence enough to satisfy the reality of my minds eye
No tweet or meme shall be exalted as gospel without due critique
Give a fuck about your rep in the streets
If what leaves your mind is not categorically concrete
Same applies to the suits and the ties
Your title cannot be vital if there is no sense in the words you provide

I'm not even aggy
I just want to highlight that you
The lover of music and words
Have allowed the standard of your diet to slide
Fast food was not designed to satisfy your appetite
I recommend a plate of your grandma's food
Mannish water or ital stew
From when you love your body
This McDonalds and chicken and chips just will not do
It, will, not, do
Free the real, free the real
Your palate is your palate and we all have a preference
But for the sake of good writing and good music
Please do not ever stop asking questions
Free the real, free the motherfucking real

My Drum

My drum requires no amplification
It can be heard if you listen intently
And it will roar if you try to ignore
I do not like shouting to be heard
As such, whilst I whisper
You can hear my drum go to work
Feel me before you hear me
And better placed you will be to hear these words

I bring offerings of good vibrations
Served with a side of funk
Expose your aura so we may communicate
Through Poetry over lunch
Insofar nothing changes
Under current conditions
I envision the beat of this drum
To be our choice of munch

Dumph Dumph

Feel me, feel me!
Feel me like changes in atmosphere
Feel me like the lover you need near
But is never quite there
Feel me like fingers through hair
Like flour and water
Kneaded with love and care
Feel me like Grandma's food

Feel me like my brothers feel Willie Lynch's noose
Feel me like the caged bird feels free
Feel me through the B-E-A-T
Of my drum

Familiarise yourself with my funk
Let us dance on open flames
Decorating the landscape with our footprints
Care free, lively
At one, with the drum
Feel the rhythm of my beat
Flow with me into the cordial of jamdown
Swirl your limbs so genteel
Then, the more you feel
I want you to while out
Within the funk there is nowhere to hideout
Buss unu style out and FUNK

Ears can only hear so much
Plus those who can't hear must feel
So take that sense data
And those internal emotions you know to be so real
Allow it to congeal
And whip you into a frenzy
For what can be learnt through the heart
But not the head?
I swear to you, it is plenty

Listen to my drum at work
Feel me before you hear me
Better placed you will be to digest these words
Feel me before you hear me
Better placed you will be to digest these words

Time Is Not Promised

Why you moving like your time is promised?
As though your expiry date is prearranged agreed and guaranteed
with the deity in charge of creating you?
News Flash!
You are not that fucking important
The Sun must set and the Sun must rise
However you dear reader are more than welcome to die
Grass will still grow, rivers will still flow
The Sun will still make space for the Moon every night

And to further dwindle our self righteous over estimated self
importance in life
As far as I can see within my minds eye
The Sun, Moon and stars are too, eligible to die
No given time of stay, no contract to honour
No guarantee that the stars will remain alight
There isn't a god damn thing on this planet that knows when its time
will be called
So please for the love of God, what are you moving like your time is
promised for?

Don't be afraid to put in work
To get up and make it count
Furthermore, if you're in a job that isn't working for you
Stop working fi dem!
Find your slice and grind like your middle name is Big Brem
Grind and joog and hustle my friend
I say grind and joog and hustle my friend
Because time elapsed is opportunity passed
And there is no getting it back my friend
In case I had not made it clear already
Your time and future are not promised
But you have the gift of the present right now
I'm just being honest

So tell me again
Why are you moving like your time is promised?

Forward

Sometimes, things don't move very fast
That's okay
Slow down
The peregrine looks at the pigeon like 'Bro!'
'You're slow!'
But when the pigeon is on a mission
Looks down to see people in its vision
It shakes its head to say
'Oh no oh no, never me, too slow!'

It doesn't matter how fast you go

Forward.

"I'll go any direction as long as it's forward" – David Livingston

Tek Time

I see my demons creeping
Stalking me in the shadows of smiles and success
I can see they're waiting for the Rasta man to slip up
I'm too high for that
Connected to a deeper situation
Ippa dippa dation
Pick a new nigger from the nation
To exalt
And watch default
It wont be me
They still call Ip Dip Doo
My nigger I wish it not for you
For all that money may buy you a seat at the table
But the moment you stop acting normal around the Caucasian
It's over
Wesley Sniped on the first given occasion
Niggas don't make it out the ghetto
We just make a little change and try let go
Unu can't escape what you know
From I born and grow my grandma taught me tek time
As a young black man, you can't afford to step out of line
Especially if you want to buss stage
Because while you're up front
They set that trap door right behind
Don't slip young Jigga

Florilegium

You don't have to be in the limelight to be in sight of the scope
Tek time young Jigga
Those bumper and breast might satisfy your smutty mind
But tek time young Jigga
It is not everybody you are to bring back to your watering hole
These bitches are not your friends
They just might tell what they know
Worst still, a whole bunch of things they don't
Protect your sovereignty whilst you bake your bread
Don't slip for some cheap thrills and quick head
That poontang could be made of gold
Don't let that be the reason you get caught out
Stay sharp young Jigga
I, like so many, want to see you rise
But there are those who will value you
Only as far as your tabloid entertainment will provide
Rise up mi dargy!
But tek time young Jigga
Remain unscathed
And in the hearts of white folk across the landscape

Tek time young Jigga.

.45

I got a 45 for the 45th
Remington, 1875
And I'm pressing pressing pressing
I got 45 for the 45th

I got a 45 for the 45th
The white house is fortified
But Doughmore Bay on an overcast day
Is the perfect place to catch corn between the eyes
Bow! I got a 45 for the 45th

It only happens to let off six
But this four five is all I need
To keep the revolution alive
I got a 45 for the 45th

I work with no accomplice
It's just me and this long tip
I wont ask for forgiveness
I got a 45 for the 45th

I hope they put his face on a penny
I'm talking to the many
Don't pray for me
I got a 45 for the 45th

If it so happens that I fail
Play this to the next
Some things you cannot curtail
I got a 45 for the 45th

Florilegium

Upon receipt of this piece
They will most probably ban me from the country
That's okay, Doughmore Bay is but ten hours away
I got a 45 for the 45th

All things return to balance before a tip of the scale
I pray this motherfucker neither weeps nor wails
That ship has long set sail
I got a 45 for the 45th

I got a 45 for the 45th
Remington, 1875
And I'm pressing pressing pressing
I got 45 for the 45th

I got a 45 for the 45th
The white house is fortified
But Doughmore Bay on an overcast day
Is the perfect place to catch corn between the eyes
Bow! I got a 45 for the 45th

Seek

Find peace
Find still
Find calm
Find serenity

Find forgiveness
Reject sickness
Of the body
And of the mind

Find joy
Find purpose
Find wealth
In health

Find a little
Find more
Share plenty
For no score

Find out why
Find a way
Show others
Together maintain

'More important than being good, is getting better'

- The Orator

'Time is our greatest enemy – not its scarcity but its abundance. We live as though we'll never die, we act as if tomorrow is promised'

- The Orator

Poetry Will Be Free

Running through the streets
Screaming Poetry will be free!
Poetry will be free!
And the Poets shall eat well
For when Poetry is freed
It shall not be free
To the pauper, it shall command your attention
To the able bodied it shall command action
To the industry it shall command your money
Because as far as rewards go
Your money is but a fraction
And the humble poet is not yet immune to bills

If you see me running through the streets
Screaming, poetry will be free!
Poetry will be free!
Do not gasp in shock
I'd prefer you asked who is this poetry?
And of what are they guilty?
I shall respond, Poetry is free!
Poetry is free and has changed the world for an eternity
This is the charge of which they find it guilty
Nonetheless – Poetry is free
Poetry is free!
Second only to ideas in the potency of its application
Carried by the minds and mouths of nomads and vagrants
Fear not of this powerful cadence
Do not make the word your enemy
Instead lend but a minute and an ear

As there is so much to be taken
Poetry is a giver and Poetry is patient
A vehicle for the knowledge of ancient
In recent times this gift of the divine
Has found itself handled by those
Who really have got it mistaken
Poetry was shackled and chained by the victors
Maimed by men of white hue with traditional English names
John, Dick and William did as much for Poetry
As the luddites did for the industrial age
For the sake of self preservation
These traditional men of traditional names
Almost acted as an inhibitor of Poetry's natural state
Growth, growth and the proclamation of change
Instead – it was never said
But through act proclaimed
Poetry lives in hardback
It's essence enclosed in black ink stains
Its prison a book shelf
No different to having the artist themselves caged
Some may argue this is the only way to preserve great works
For the future they are too concerned
It is today we hone the ability
To create and generate combinations of words
That will today or tomorrow change the earth
Poetry is free - left only on bookshelves to die
It has always been so and always will be so – you needn't ask why
As long as poetry remains a collection of reflections within the lives
of you and I
Poetry will be free

…. But it's a fuck you and pay me to the industry

Twenty Six

I'm the same age as Big L at the time of his passing
I am less than 12 months away from the passing of Pac
Time is passing me by
Like the air you breathe
It's not something you can grasp
I see these men as my peers
My classmates and comrades
Each assigned a higher duty
Though forgive me as I'm forced to compare
The days we did not share
I don't care much for like-for-like comparisons
My expectations are real, I can manage them
But not always the misery that plagues my thought processes invisibly
What will they write in my obituary?
What will they read in my absence?
Will they cherry pick best moments?
And fasten a cloak for my memory to don?
Or will they do me honourably and honestly like I lived?
Come right or wrong?
Truth be told – I won't be here to find out
During this short tenure be assured
That I'll be the last one to scream and shout
About whatever 'successes' I've got going down

Let us make this clear
I am living in fear
In 12 months I will have outlived Biggie
And by my own standards I think that shit is mad
This lends to why I feel it bad
The pressures of being a good human being
In a world that has gone mad
The pressures of parenthood when I'm not yet a dad
The pressures of the block, they never get old
It was only last year that I was on the way to Paris
When I heard my younger brother had been stabbed
Naturally my thoughts went all black everything
And a hundred mile journey and back
But listen, whilst I'm happy to restore the balance
Facts are facts
Me sitting in prison would be as much out of place
As a passa passa rave for man in drag
So… if I must gwarn wicked and bad
Let it be with this pen, and this pad
Fleshing out open wounds and scabs
I give it to you raw
The healing is the sharing
Higher powers perhaps
I'm grateful for the time I have
And at a loss for my brothers amiss
I never claimed to be able to save them all
But I'll try to shine a little light in their iris
I only ask that you read this over my grave if I die before 26
Read this over my grave if I die before 26

Peace

How about it?
Peace for a day
Don't shout it
Just tell every third person
You see on your way

How about it?
Peace for a day
Don't shout it
Just tell every third person
You see on your way

Tertiary

Focus on the tertiary is certainly irking me
Absurdities in the third degree purposely served to me
All for the words…

'Yeah, you're hard'
Like lard, like dairylea

Fuck a wave
Motion in the ocean keep it slick like lotion
Devotion through commotion means your notion is potent
Hold on! Amen

I'm too evolved for laws central or devolved to keep a hold
Still though, many cold souls ten toes on road
With no hope dough or droe progress is slow so bro stick to what he
know
But how do you grow if you stick to what you know?

So I understand all this focus on the tertiary
Certainly irking me
Absurdities in the third degree
Purposely served to me
All for the words….

'Yeah, you're hard'
As long as your intention is pure
Yeah G, you are.

Ruckus

It's time we do away with the notion that Poets don't do commotion
We aren't all vegan cokeheads talking bare happy go lucky poems
Some of us are really out here!
On the forefront of life's fuckeries
Throwing caution to the wind
So we may spin you some motherfucking realness
I'm not happy with 'just' making you grin
The transfer of ideas needs nurturing
So amma give you something to take with you
Nay do I kid you
Hold a sec, hold a thought
Hold an idea, maybe more
Flesh will wither, memory cards will fail
Even with a tribe begotten
I'm told it takes three generations for a name to be forgotten
So in my innings, whether losing or winning
I'll always give you more than nothing
And pray you receive the immaterial gems sent your way
Ideas live forever
But remember your name will fade away

P.S Don't @ Me

I'm a young jiggy brother
I'm a hella jiggy yute
I speak in wholes
And lambaste in broad speaking truths
Dear white people
Some of you get my fucking nerves sometimes
God's honest truth
It's not always some cultural appropriation fuckery
Secondary school is the first time it touched me
Five words – Do Not – Touch – My Hair
And I shouldn't have to repeat myself
But in practice I do
There's more to my irritation
Holding it back is not something I can do
Stop screw up your rarseclart face when you hear a poem
You know damn well isn't for you
That blank expression is starting to tickle my not-so-funny bone
Spare me time dear reader to tell you how it goes
I open my mouth and begin
The cadence and vocabulary lures them in
Then the blackness starts to leak out
Resulting in their body language morphing
The more I keep talking
I see this mind boggling contortion spread

Florilegium

Faces no longer so heavily invested in what they understood but five
lines ago
The mention of anything overtly negro
IS an immediate no go
All of a sudden the audience can no longer follow
No longer make sense of what they perfectly knew but a few lines ago
Just because it's not for you doesn't warrant the fuckery I see at some
of my shows
Please re to the fucking lax
Not all literature in this bastard tongue was made to satisfy your
literary angst
Give thanks that you can understand me when I'm vex
As much as you allow yourself to understand
I speak in your tongue and write in your hand
But dear white people, not everything was made for the middle class
white man
There are narratives you may scorn at
Or see as out of hand
But you dear white people do not get to dictate the narrative of this
man
Or any other
2020 it's a new programme
The host is black
The narrative too
Everything about this is black
And if that should make you uncomfortable
You are free to leave this room
But we will no longer be muting the truth
Muting our truth
Black is beautiful, powerful and requires witnesses
It is at this juncture I invite you

Hotep

The Prettiest Nitty

I saw a flame almost die
I see a spark that will not yet roar
When you see her, try not to scorn
Hope and well wishes cannot pay the debt that dreams afford
And we're all broke
Some of us in different ways
I don't know her name
But I know her face
In her eyes I can see a life long devoid of praise
Why the wind blows is not important
However, you name one person that doesn't want the wind in their sails
See the wind it whistles the wind it wails
Now I invite you to witness the shadow it casts over the flame
Until it is lights out
It will flicker and flicker until it can burn bright again
I know it burns baby but push back the shade
So you might shine
When you see her coming to ask you for a change
Don't be blind
Afford her the time
If you must – be polite in your decline
We are all people – it costs nothing to be kind
I wrote this for the prettiest nitty
I can't say for sure that she'll be fine
But I'll be so happy to see her flame burn bright again
To the prettiest nitty

Spiritual Brew

Mad sick, head nuh good
The pen doth kiss page
Whilst the mouth do tell
Wizard whispers
Each sentence is the casting of a spell
My poetic sisters cook up a bitches brew
Served wholesomely each and every time
They bestow upon us their presence
Poetic presents they gift us
Recollections of life experiences
Spun into odes of gold
As if told to be legend in the heavens
We are thinkers – the word is our weapon
We meditate in preparation for the toil that beckons
We burn the wick at both ends so
It may be possible to write
In solitude
And contribute at the coming together of the wise
Unilaterally unidentified congregations of builders,
teachers, activists and dinner ladies
Offer ideas to collide
On street corners
At after school clubs
Barbershops
Super market shopping isles
In this room right now and outside

They speak in poetry
Their truth equivalent to verse
For poetry is the language of thinkers
Prior to any science, there was the word
Great minds spend their time in thought
Greater minds spend their time in thought and rhyme
For how effective is the message
If it cannot be digested by the recipient?
All hail the glorious magnificent
Power of the word
Blessed are those who step to the plate
When asked if they identify as one of the greats
Aye, I indeed identify as a Poet
My oath is as follows

I do solemnly decree
First – To be the greatest version of myself possible

Second – To be a beacon of honesty and righteousness
Despite the fact, it might just be the end of me

Third – I will live, die, prosper and falter by my word

Fourth – I will recognise, represent, elevate and energise
The history and depth of the word

Fifth – I solemnly decree I will live my life and represent the
times and tales with honesty and integrity

Call The Cartographer

Where can I rest my head free from the ills of the world?
Where is it that I can eat the fruit of the harvest I did not sow?

Oh where be it that I can be so fat but so poor?
And so rich but have accumulated no wealth?

Where is it that all men be recognised as free?
Where is that place which all are free
To exercise their sovereignty over consciousness?
We have longed for this

Where is it that the .45's are still made of shellac?
Where shells are found only on the beach?

It's the co-ordinates to the place where they've done away with
equality that I need
Replaced with fairness
A place where every child, woman and man
Is guaranteed a feed

Does such a place exist?
And if it did, where would it be?
Probably, for the time being
Only in the hearts of you and of me

Breathe

Breathe with me dargy
Breathe
Will you leave with me dargy?
Eeeeee?
Extract peace with me dargy
From the midst of all this grief
'round us dargy

I plea with thee to take leave from the madness

History

Teach me to read your history
At the expense of my own
Teach me to read your history
I will pay the fee
You may keep the cost unknown
If you teach me to read your history
I should elevate to the ranks of intellectual
Enabled to contribute to the global society
Teach me to read your history
So I may explore great stories
Of valour, to humanity to democracy
To saving savages from their insanity
Grant me the ability to retrace the steps of the victor
So I too, may share in the spoils
Give me a seat at the table
In fact, my audacity has grown so
That I now demand a seat at the table
Serve me from no wooden spoon
I will be served from silver, like you
For I am a student of your history
A disciple of your house
So you will feed me and treat me as such

Of course this was never to be
Those who have studied the course of their history
Can tell you – it is theirs
They will rightfully, forever and always be
The centre piece
Study the history of the white man
But at no point beg from it a piece
The ink has long since dried on the deal to teach us your history
We are neither grateful nor pleased
But we are here
Raising fists, and taking knees
Writing our history in the language
Of the one time – long time enemy

City Lights

The night sky reveals the flutter of filaments
Reds and whites dart across inroads
Carved carefully into the concrete landscape
Queues of trains glow across the upper terraces of the skyline
Hot potato wrapped in yesterdays byline
Provides subsistence for the night walkers
Street workers and temporarily hushes the slick talkers

In the absence of foreground kerfuffle
The city silence rolls loudly
By tower blocks, crop grows, brooks and jetties
You've got to love the city
Boss man's cold drinks are lukewarm
Man dem love to watch gyal
But getting your head buss over one is petty
Keep wise about yourself when under city lights
A city without fault is a city without fight
We'll get back to that in the morning
For tonight we tread steadfast
Live slow
And appreciate these city lights

Firm Ground

Make no enemy of chance
Prepare for war only on the basis of sound and confirmed actions
To express anger on stage
Is by no means a gentleman's fashion
Grant no man the power to draw you out
Allow no unworthy man to feel force of forearm holding stout
Give no eedyat a piece of your mind
Especially if you see no peace in conversing with his

Make no enemy of chance
Presumed burden of stress manifest
Hidden from flesh
But rooted in our chest
This is your life alie?
Then grant no battyhole permission to test
Make no enemy of chance
Prepare for war only on the basis of sound and confirmed actions
To express anger on street
Is by no means a gentleman's fashion

Carrie

I stand by the bay of the water
It's cold
I tremble and shiver
(Carrie Run! Carrie Run! Go Now!)

I dip my toe into the baltic lake
I find myself knee deep
And I begin to weep
Until the waters reach my bosom
(Run! Run Carrie, Run!)

But I can't run any further
The cold finds it's way into my bones
Stiffness surges through limbs
It begins
I shall die alone
Choking under the weight of tears

Wash me away wash me away
Wash me away wash me away
Wash me away wash me away

And like that
Her final prayer was answered
Pass this on today
So tomorrow they will pray
For little Carrie who was carried by the bay

Never Ignorant
Getting Goals Accomplished

They will not tell you, I am *that* nigger
They will tell you I am not he
They will tell you that there are no niggers
They will tell you, we're all niggers

They will not tell you, I am that nigger
For if they tell you I am he
The price on my life doubles
And the sheep will have to flee

The chameleons will be outed and ousted
This here nigger is really about it
Honeysome danger is the flavour
Served in this dish of niggerish behaviour

Niggers do exist
White people don't see them until its too late
Black people are still on the fence regarding the public debate

But niggers remain
I'm glad to say their population is on the decline
Minds pollinated are harder to contain
Whilst ignorant black folk are harder to find
The spirit of the nigger will exist until the end of time
To deny me this would be a sacrilegious crime

Then again, none of that is the most important thing you need to know about me.

My Son

My son will have no roof
Glass ceilings are of no use
Views misconstrued
You see bluntness as crude
But we see a son rise once in a blue moon

Howl howl! Hooty hoo!
My son will have no roof
Lion cubs stay cute
But by the hairs on my maney mane mane
My son will have roof

UoB Intertextuality

Neutron stars amuse at the bells and whistles spouted by their fatal
attraction
Gravitational waves ebb and flow between the two bodies
In a constant universal glue
They know nothing of each other
Their minds tangled upon the vine of intellectual thoughts expressed
by meter of creative mess
The same vine that would place them slap bang together
If only for twelve months of their time within the time space
continuum
This coming together will nay last forever
But without doubt it will produce gold

How Are You Today?

I am the sculpted beauty of human excellence
Courageous and bold
Timid and weak
You undress me with your eyes
But care not for my head or feet
My thoughts irrelevant to yours
And I cannot run
A slave to your desires
As it conspires, it was never black or white
The stroke of your gaze
Enough to make my chest vibrate
But I cannot run
Beauty be a curse
Summed up in these words
Words I cannot say
Body language depraved of free expression
Simply because of the technicolour dream coat I call pride
That coats my shame
And makes fools of your eyes
This is not a beautiful painting

Dawn

Was there peace on the dawn of war?
Were dorm mice nipping through fields
Or scuttling between floor boards?
Does the reaper take the night off
In preparation for the work ahead?
Fields lay still – wild life play dead
The sun will rise with a sad brow today
For many many fathers will take one to the head
At least, it seems
There is peace on the dawn of war.

Clap

They   clapping   they   clapping   they   clapping
They   clapping   they   clapping   they   clapping
They clapping

So I'm running and I'm ducking
And I'm bobbing and I'm weaving
Trying to hit the deck
Before my soul hits the ceiling

Cah they clapping they clapping they clapping
They clapping they clapping they clapping
They wont stop until they hit
Lord forgive Lord forgive
They might try sacrifice me to the crimson tide
On god, I can't die tonight

So keep clapping keep clapping keep clapping keep
clapping
And I'll keep writing
So keep clapping
Clap at me or clap for me, clap with me
Again for the young Queens
Clap with me
One time for life
Clap with me
Again for the time you almost broke
Clap with me
I pray you carry love I pray you carry peace
I pray you carry love I pray you carry peace
Clap with me, for me or at me
I pray you carry love I pray you carry peace

A 3am Walk

Heartstrings pulsate and bulge beyond the cavity beneath my left breast
Walking 'til my feet burn but heaven is a mile away
And I smell death
Don't try to hold your breath
Take it in
Buss a grin
Hear the angels sing from beyond the mist
Hone in
Knowing if heaven was but a mile away
Right here in the shoes you wear
Is the closest moment you'll have
Wear it proud
Angels loud
Love in my heart
Strings pulsating and bulging beyond the cavity beneath my left breast
And as said
I can find no enemy in the stench of death

So I keep walking
Keep walking keep walking
(And I grin)
And keep walking

H.N.I.C

I am the head nigger in charge
Contrary to popular belief
What you see is not what you get
Upon receipt of a laboured sigh of relief
Just when you think it's safe again
I move swiftly to remind you that I
Only I am the Head Nigger In Charge
Legal, employment and social structures
Have made sure outspoken black folk are not the norm
All while we remain over subscribed to mental health wards and dorms
Throughout our communities we often hear
'So and so has been locked up and they've thrown way the key'
So I'm an antagonist to the state
But if you need the story in reverse
From cradle to hearse
They had got my number before I was attributed a name
I was never meant to be jack shit
Explore for thyself, the statistics remain
Niggers will always be Red
Maybe hired to play dead but never Andy Dufrane
The sky will bleed before I allow that shit to wash
Live and let be
Routinely objectify and test me
Either way, I will stake my claim
To the name, Head Nigger In Charge
I will make my bed in the house
But sleep under the stars
I will cook for the village
But be sure to eat last
I will perform the duties expected of me

And all others I reasonably can
I will represent on committees
Alien to that we have seen at home
I will brush shoulders with soldiers
And lay with those who rest their head upon stone
I will be the rebel music
The morning drum to your morning run
When in distress
I will be your flare gun
I'm the monkey to make the circus master jump
Hand out forty lashings
Spill a little red rum
For I am the head nigger in charge
All fassyhole fascists better run
I am the head nigger in charge
And I march with an army of one

No Social Class

The negro has no social class
Doth thy cap to those
Who commit to finding logic in the absence of sense
Absent fathers repent to their sons
For their absence in the past
Though can't form the bonds that they miss
Damn near not knowing what a father son bond is
Simultaneously championing the myth
That he is somehow raising a king
Inept to the art of child rearing
Still charting stories of passing on knowledge of depth
To the seed he claims is 'next'
Next to be like you brother?
Next to make something from the streets?
Next bona fide hustler?
Juggling everything except for his fatherhood responsibilities
Nah, our seed will be far greater than we
Sitting on a hundred bag don't make you a rich dad
Staying home to raise your kids doesn't make you a poor dad
Water and feed your seed all the knowledge they need
Raise the mast and fly the flag
Build your own because at the end of the day
The nigger has no social class

Do You Know Your Wrongs?

The biggest killer of young inner city men, is pride
The silent killer
It's nothing to do with hyper masculinity
This isn't a poem about the block
More so about maintaining peace
When a likkle fassy just will not stop.
Some men die over nothing
That is merely one side
Some men are rude and disrespectful
Some men have a difficult time letting it slide
A good man with a good plan to do bad things
Can be a worrying sight
So we chant denounce evil and holla reject badness from life
Situations will arise where a fassy will test your resolve
Going against everything you show people that you're about
Some men are like this
Serving no purpose but to test your clout
5 word for dem likkle bumbahole deh
You Cannot Draw Me Out
I'd rather spin you a line than waste my time
And have you be the reason I act out of pride
Some men are nice because it is in their nature
Some men are nice because it is better that way
Don't let pride be the reason you die
Or the reason you tek life
The biggest killer of inner city men
Is nothing to do with hyper masculinity
And everything to do with knowing wrong from right

Ruby Red Day

A rare condition keeps my eyes red
Characterised by lack of sleep
It's go hard or dead
I'm the owner of ruby red eyes
Bespeckled with white lies
But you never know what's what with my delivery
I happily sacrifice my time to spend a little in your company
Jolts of 'ohh noo' surge through my body when you're touching me
A man isn't meant to receive his full blessing at once
You don't even understand what's going on
Or maybe you do?
Waiting for me to speak up
And I love how you think I'm that fucking strong
Plucking at these fucking heart strings
I'll play you a symphony for one
And if I compose a note telling you of all the things that couldn't be
more right
I fear the response couldn't be more wrong
So it's more code, more hearing things unsaid
More indoors – hold me close

More keep it cold when we do road
And I don't know
If a brother needs any more
A brothers needs are a brothers needs
But a brother's pleased if you hold the champion score
Champion bubbler
Champion bubble on this muddle once more
Let me hold you close until the show close
Then I'll encore once more
I'll have to die on stage for all
Before this love hits the floor
I got ruby red eyes
I'm not lovesick for shit
But I'm convinced you're the cure

Uhmm Hmm

Back to front
Back to love
Over tears
We stroll across
Via tear ducts
To firmer ground

HATE

Shatter, shudder, thrust 'n' bawl

Equinox dawns, the blood still fresh

The quivers can't shake the goose bumps

Alone, far removed from peace

He took the last of that

In his first grasp

She blew what would be her last

Innocent breath

With it

Leaving behind all she knew of trust

Mobilise

There are matters on subjects
Of which I feel I've said all I can
Before we get carried in conversations had a thousand times
It's time we changed the narrative
To action, reaction and root our factions in plan
Aunty, mummy, scammer and gunman
Mobilise your family, friends and gang
Reject laying low when it's possible to stand
Blood must boil
When for your toils
One receives only scraps of the spoils

When the job you work will not pay for the products you sell
Rampage
When you watched dozens burn to death in Grenfell
Rampage
Then when you're told there are nearly eighty deaths to tell
Rampage
Hella fucking rampage

I'm a writer, well aware of my slice
Sweat on brow, weapon in hand
I'm still two stepping on the front line
Tired of talking
I'm ready to shove my blue bookies pen in an enemies swallow pipe
Tek time before the meek have nothing to eat
And we're forced to tek life

And I'm not going to have this conversation a thousand times

Keep writing

Florilegium

Big Zoots and Biscuits

The Everyday Struggle

Every day I try take leave from the misery
To rise with the sun
So I can provide for my son
Literally doing everything I can
To stay above the water
Standing firmly on my shoulders
Is my daughter
So excuses are not an option
Mr-make-a-way so I must can make a way
I'm Mr-make-a-way so I must can make a way

Wool

I have hair like wool
And will like water

I have hair like wool
And will like water

17 Slaves

African men are being sold as slaves
I repeat
African men are being sold as slaves
Today
You are not alone in your temporary mutism
Grey smog will not bellow from the rolls of green
Tony Gallagher will not stop the press
Neither May nor Merkle will take platform like Macron
Neither one has or will, make national address
The current US administration
Will not consider invading in the name of democracy
Much less an official letter of solidarity bearing hallmark and crest
You are definitely not alone in your mutism
The US has a vested interest in keeping its mouth shut
We can't forget that Libya was stable and able
Prior to Muammar's death
Look yah now
Military intervention from the west
Nurtured a country flawed but doing its best
To be an incubator of slavery and death
How things change
But shit remains the same
£400 for a full-grown slave
And not ten pence worth of ink is used to highlight it on a front page
Black Lives Matter
To the value of £400
It seems they matter most to those willing to pay
Bare a thought to the notion
That if a fifty strong volunteer group from the UK
Was abducted and sold within a matter of days
The British government would be all the rage

Florilegium

Condolences from state leaders would reign
And I haven't even mentioned the word slave
Follow me to twitter if you may
#PrayForLibya why??
That denotes to the unbeknownst
That it is Libyans for whom we should pray
Raising awareness is great
But the root of that phrase
Comes from terrorist attacks
Whereby all is said and done after the fact
When prayers and hindsight dominate the chat
Please pray for the situation in Libya
But this is not yet after the fact
So prayer without action is a whole lot of meaningless chat
Get the fuck up and act
Do what you can
Tell whom you know
Evil must succumb when the balance of positivity begins to grow
Pray yes, act also
Tweet, pray for Libya
Say it in the real world more so
There are men for sale in Africa
It is uncomfortable to know once that sits in your dome
There are Black Men for sale in Africa
Miraculous how a colour can soften the blow
Tell somebody to tell somebody
Keep raising awareness as you go
This is a battle for the men and women of good
We don't need the UN going full gung-ho
Men and women of good
Raise your voice for freedom as you go
Relay, that there are men for sale in Africa
It should not sit well with the audience of the globe
But.... There aren't any white men for sale
Now ask yourself if that softens the blow

WAR

We make sex like war
Incense and Lemon Diesel
Rest in the bosom of my trojan horse
Bring me unto your warmth
Welcome me with nipples pointing skyward
Arms stretched and breast buoyant
I will follow your lead
Knee deep into the trenches
Suddenly seizing opportunity
To lay you face down
Knead deep into the crevice at the small of your back
We play Beres to disguise the sounds
The sounds you make whilst your face contorts
Muscles spasm and contract
There will be no release for the time being
I'mma keep you bound
As I dig down
For you, are my, prisoner of war

The Dojo

Experiences such as this are rare in the gossip group chats
They don't make love like us
That's just the way it is
They don't fuck like us
And that's how it goes
They wont understand the surges
Surging from head to toe
The dominant command over your body shown
They don't experience love in the physical like we do
Safe words mean nothing until you endure
A little more of this boiling rage
Embroiled in a dangerous game
On the brink of destroy or create
Suspended over the edge of the bed
At the end of your wick
In full knowledge that the way we make love
Is enough to make your nastiest friend sick
We work in the dojo
Demanding dedication during the dicking
Don't decide you're done
Or dare decide to run
The dojo we play in
Is not a place of childish fun

It's where we harbour tension
To release its frustration
In the direction
Of your Yoni and my hood
In the absence of love
It is still made on dressers
Dining room tables, soft backs and hardwood
In body language we talk nuff
Words vacate at the taste of these two fingers in your mouth
About to make your insides cark up
Twiss up and stretch
Not to give away the play
However before the end of what is left
You will feel me in your chest
And whom will you tell?
The group chat will categorise this as gas
Facts
Your girl, the one who be the self proclaimed freak of the week
Don't even be dishing out game like that
I hope you're too wicked in fact
To share any of this, with anyone

Incoming flashbacks
Knees crumbling, back blown
Legs collapse
Flashbacks
Whiplash
Can't run, legs cramp
Flashbacks
To bring that up mid conversation
Or slide that in the group chat is madness

Florilegium

74

In practice, remember
Bawl if you must but don't run
I'll go slow if you need a rest, but don't run
Inhibitions are suppressed
The dojo becomes the sacred sight of sanctified fun
I suspect a warm welcome when you cum
Down from our ethereal place of play
Welcome to the dojo
The physical manifestation of your favourite domains

Rubin Carter

Will they Rubin Carter me?
Will the echoes of Rubin Carter's downfall
And subsequent rise
Be repeated in the cycle of my life?

If the most notable order of the garter
Was bestowed upon my family name
Would I still be the subject of relentless hate?
A hate sown into the fabric of society
Engrained and pressed
Under the weight of a scolding iron

I choose to adorn my skin with this fabric
It is not brushed
Nor is it comfortable to the pores of my skin
It is very far from the gansey of invisibility it was sold to me as
This fabric, this blasted fabric of hate wears like chainmail
Bloody uncomfortable
Blood dribbles pedantically through the cold linkages
Disguising the chaffing, which tears through my epidermis
I chose to wear this tunic
A conscious decision to fit in the social frameworks
Provided to me by the powers that be
But a hurricane wears no clothes
A hurricane is beautiful, natural and has no foes

Florilegium

Items in a hurricanes path
Will be flattened on impact
Neither the fool nor the academic
Will lay blame at the feet of the hurricane for that
The hurricane must be free
Naked as naked can be
I harbour the truth in my eye
And there's a high wall of fuckery
Protecting the hurricane from what you think it should be
I'm Rubin Carter in '63
Fuck that, I'm Rubin Cater in '67
Fuck that, I'm Rubin Carter aged 11
Fuck that, my name is the hurricane
And a hurricane is beautiful

Gallows

Heads will roll and folks will line up by the gallows in there thousands
As sure as the stars that glow, heads will roll
On our final night we pray the wick burns slow
That the darkness is slow gentle in its pace
That the ticking of the clock will continue after the judge has called
time on my case
Bury me on the top floor of the estate
Plant Sativa on my grave
Smoke up knowing that it's the ideas
They can take ownership of my physical cage
With the belief that in death I no longer remain
They may take it, all
I rarely spent time in my frame anyway
It's the ideas that pertain to an existence
Beyond what can be obtained by sense data
As I prepare for conversations with the creator
I pray the wick burns slow
And long enough for me to become familiar with the roads leading to
the gallows
For as sure as the stars that glow
Heads will roll
And folks will line up by the gallows in there thousands

Don't Turn Your Back

Don't turn your back on me niggah
Don't turn your back on me niggah
With all that academic vigour
You think you can turn your back on me niggah?
Get the fuck outta here with that shit
If you hit the belly we'd still go halves on a brick
Don't turn your back on me niggah
I used to feed you
Picked you up when they decided to leave you
You can't turn your back on me niggah
I held you up when them dumb fucks fell like autumn leaves
Don't you dare turn your back on ME niggah
I'm the air you breathe
Go forth and achieve
But turn your back on me niggah
There won't be any reason to breathe niggah
Try me
Niggah
You built me up to this
Niggah
Brick by brick you built me to protect you from the jungle
I was there the first time you got your dick sucked
Gave you cover the first time you got ran down by feds
Was the first to show you real bread
Hardough, hard food
Niggah you owe your culture to who?

Turn your back on me niggah
I dare you turn your back on me niggah
I'll burn your whole set down like Samuel Sharpe
You family darg
But turn your back on me
Turn your back on me niggah?
You might meet my mate Stanley
And he don't really like niggas
So don't bother try niggah
Sit down and rideee niggah
Cuz you can't ever turn your back on me
NIGGAH.

Raised Up

I was raised on Killamanjaro, Black Cat and Ram Jam Rodigan
Read it again
I was raised on Crazy Titch, Ruff Sqwad and Newham Generals
I was raised on C Dash, Rezz G and the D Hart Mega Mix
I got dubs for the weak heart and anybody trying a ting
I can't tek back chat nor carry man like a sling

I was raised on Killamanjaro, Black Cat and Ram Jam Rodigan
Read it again
I was raised on Crazy Titch, Ruff Sqwad and Newham Generals
I was raised on C Dash, Rezz G and the D Hart Mega Mix
I got dubs for the weak heart and anybody trying a ting

WOOP WOOP
WAKE UP

Wake up sleeping Negros
Shake off the slumber
Rub the nymapi from your eyes
Woop Woop! Wake up Nigga
The time is now
Your calling be that voice in your head
Respond nigga
Wash your crotches
Make your bed
Rub the nyampi from your eyes
Double take
Rub your neck back
Read between the lines
Toast and butter that breadback
Be grateful for the little you have
Give thanks
Play ball
Shake hands
Kiss arse
Quash your plans
Whatever you do
To make it though today niggah
Let them know you have surrendered your mask
Do not apologise and do not relapse
Rub the nyampi from your eyes
On my life
Today we all face the facts

Do What It Do

Birds must swim, Fish must fly
The odds of success are high
Insofar you are not too smart
And your mouth not too bright

Trying to hoover last night's drugs out the rug
No longer high as a kite
You realise
Birds must swim, fish must fly
At some point we all ride the 16:55
To a 6pm sunrise

Say Something Please

It's easy to say nothing
Populating scores of lines not designed
To enrich the lives of the reader
Is neither here nor there

Write for, and about that which you may spare care
Write, recite, memorise words said
Offer your sixpence, pull up a chair
Fine dine on water and bread

Funny how the poor man is the first to share
In a world where not even the most entitled flesh
Can be carried forward from thy deathbed

Butterflies

Butterflies flicker in the haze of the sunlight
Flight patterns lay grace above the site of last nights knife fight
Mothers will and have cried
It will take the ground £500 of public money
And three winters to lose its newly dressed shade of red
And we as a nation ask why?

The butterflies keep up their dance
Dressed in glistening sunlight
If done right
The essence of the soul passed to the other side
Is imprinted to the wings of a juvenile butterfly
The most senior take charge of the ceremony
Conducting convulsions of spirit
To the rhythm of life for the last time
Now, surrendered for a glance of what lies ahead
As a life force transcends, a door is closed
And before dust is made of bone
The wandering shall find home
Upon the wings of a butterfly
A juvenile, itself too, lost
Guided by the guardians to explore a world of loss
Matched up with a spirit at odds
With being ethered by the reaper
Before he could become king to his young gods
Only the butterflies can help him progress from this loss
If his redemption is to be published to the wings of a juvenile
It might just give the butterfly enough lift to see the world anew
May its perspective skew
When the world is viewed from aloft

Carry spirit to the heavens Mr Butterfly
Look down as you rise above
Entrust your unspent blessings to your young gods
As well as others you love
£500 and three winters from now
They will have washed away the last of your blood
I wrote this to inform others about the truth in your demise
The truth about the butterflies
The truth in knowing the dead don't die
… Until we let them
This is why I see your eyes on the back of every other butterfly
In the summertime I find a quite field and pour up the rum
Lay down and watch you pass me by
The dead don't die
Word to me, you and these butterflies

Money Hold Who?

Money don't hold me
Money can't grow we
Money can't mek yam grow inna ground
Currency can't always measure inna pound
Money haffi mek
But currency is debt
And to collect
Wickedness goes down
But when they lower you
Bare foot or inna shoe
Remember money can't spend inna ground
Money can't spend inna ground

I Will

Hold me in the fashion that he Bassist holds her Bass
      I will
Grip me like the drummers sticks in the midst of the tension
      I will
Make no fool of me through false promise, give me what you said you would
      I will
      If I deploy myself to the trail of your scent

I will, be waiting for soft skin and firm grip, do me right
      I will, on sight
Do not lie to me, I have never run from a fight,
      Lord knows
Do me like prince did the rock and roll hall of fame in '04
      Woman how you know about that? Tell me likkle more
I will
Do me like stormzy did the Brit Awards
      Make it rain indoors and fuck up your whole shit?
      I will
Like Marley in Zimbabwe 1980
Or MTV unplugged '01 Lauryn Hill

Florilegium

    Woman I will break you
    I have no discipline instilled
    Outing all this wickedness
    It can't be safe for you in the field

I can't be afraid
Of what? Of who? Of you?
I will make you say my name and pedicure toes

    Pause.
    How about I put you on all fours
    And see how bad you want this bone

I'm vegan

    Looooooool and I'm going home.

My Friend

My friend
Would you invade Africa – if the order was so?
I see
You, cannot answer
Would you kill your people
People that look like you?
Your mother and fathers countrymen?
Would you kill these people
If the order was so?
I see
There is no straight answer
My friend
I want to know if you would kill somebody
Somebody you did not know
For a reason you do not understand
I would then like to know the price of life
But not the cost of war
My friend
I have seen the dead
Yet I could not warn them of your arrival
I could not inform them
That a man of their same nappy appearance would break rank
To kill a brother - for a reason he does not fully understand

Florilegium

Bound by order
Severed from compassion
My friend is this right?
I see
You have no answer
It is never okay to disobey orders
Killing your brothers and sisters
Aunties and uncles
Well that is just war
And these things come with a price

My friend
The cost of living is high enough
You do not want to be in debt to the dead
At the cusp of your life

I love you dearly
My friend
The military guy

Who?

Who will defend it when they come for you?
Who will stan' up in the face of adverse authority
To defen' it for you?
Who have you stood for?
Who is it that you had to be on the run from the law for?
Interesting
Tell me more
Tell me more about the root of your cause
Describe to me a situation whereby
You'd be willing to swap your Kenzo piece
For a red cotton gauze
And another where you'd be at peace
With your corpse being pushed from the shore
What are you willing to perish for?
Once you're sure
Tell a stranger likkle more

I am the root
You may be the flower

Sometimes the window is big
Sometimes the window is small
Take care of the soil all of the time
And harvest shall be a ball

Wandering Child of Maroon Town

Wandering child of Maroon Town
Oh where have you been?
We were expecting you long before sun down
What is it that has kept you away?
Come home and tell us all you have seen
Wondering child of Maroon Town
What seeds have you sown on your wayward way home?
Anywhere we go we have to grow
Lost you may have been but we know that you know
No child is ever really severed from spirit
It's guidance will lead you away from the finite
You just have to listen to it
We know you could not draw within the lines
Take that mind and go find the lucid
Bring it with, home to Maroon town
Wandering child – no time is too long-a-while
Roots can't measure inna a mile
Any others, brothers and sisters found
Bring dem come

Forever they will be welcomed and embraced
None shall face exile
None shall be deceived like the victors of 1728
Bring dem come wandering child of Maroon Town
See it true
Through you others will place their toes on sanctified ground
Bring with you knowledge of the world when you reach
Like branches on trees
Extended towards sun light
I will prepare a heavy soup of supernal magnitude
Made with vegetables discarded as uncouth
Together we will dine by firelight
In the company of those who chose their own name
Reclaimed as family on this here day
Exalt your crown child of Maroon Town
For the elders are proud that you have found your way
Exalt your crown child of Maroon town
Be sure others can see the way

Candyman

Fighting demons
Screaming candy man candy man
Candy man throughout the fucking evening

Chicken heads want to fuck and suck
Fuck and suck the trust out of my guts
Buss my melon so they can see
Blood flow from tear ducts

Love corrupt
My heart push dust out my oesophagus
Coughing up remnants of happier times
In a gust resembling glitter crushed
Lust for being loved lift me up
Even times when I had made my bed in a rut
See my wrists, here it is, please cut
Please cut
Director don't stop but please cut
Take two if you need to
Another wrist, here it is
You don't have to ask
I'll give it up fast
Drop dead at the drop of a hat
Would you if could you, retract words given?
Knowing that the energy spewed is spent
And cannot be given back?
Poetry is crack
If I could slit my wrist
To see how much you'd miss the hit
I would do it

97

Bleed out on live stream just to see the impact
Until I find the strength
It's candyman candyman candyman
Waiting for a hook to be lodged in my head
A minor set back when you dabble in words
When you want the world to read your work
Yet can't afford to be alive
So why oh why, shouldn't I reside under
earth?
If it means I'll trend for a day
And they'll know my name
I suppose it could be worse

Bandulu

Tip toes pitter patter to the natter of drum skins
The bandulu is coming
This thief wants nothing of your bread or cheese
Dem tings dere the bandulu would leave
This bandulu is no normal thief
Gold and silver are of little consequence to he
More importantly
The bandulu would care to know
If you are able to move your feet
In a 2x2 and 4x4 kinda beat
To a rhythm
On repeat
If it is so
It is likely the bandulu you will meet
Between the tap of the toe and the kiss of the feet
Incognito the bandulu will sneak up the space between your thighs
Past the sag in your jeans
Over the crease in your neck
Lest we forget
Bandulu is thief!
And none a unu are getting away scot free
So next time you whine up
And grind up yourself inna blues
Remember the bandulu with his rucksack of hoo-doo
Is watching
Heckling, yelling 'Tek weh yuself!'
The minute that the party is done
Time doesn't fly when the I is having fun
About where did the time go?
Look good look good see the bandulu ah run
About where did the time go?
Look good look good see the bandulu a run

Alpaca Rug

Words are power
Words are power
Allow knowledge to be your fuel
Truth to be your guide
Travel to the end of your capabilities
Lay a white flag to signify that you
Are the conqueror of all that lay behind
If the trail should go from alpaca rugs to alpaca shit
Mind your step then shimmy as you skip
Keep fucking going because there's not much more to it
Knowledge – fuel
Truth – guide
Alpaca rug – Alpaca shit
Keep fucking going
Because there's not much more to it

Sunken Place

I spent nearly two weeks with my spirit unsettled
Not an easy spirit to disturb
I gave the situation the credence it deserved
Aware of my powers that tend to the play
Old decisions and new jin hoped my spirit would sway
Far enough from my physical cage to be enticed to stay
Knowing that my spirit is aged
Demons prayed I stayed long enough to slip a weight around my fate
Such was the latest attempt to make the I an ornament at the depths of the sunken place

I can pass through but I cannot stay
Visit, but not for too long and never too late
I man must rise
I man can't fool again
I man can't grant power in a space
Where spirits exude hate
I man can't depend on fate
So when I'm run down, I maintain
All things must come to pass

I don't do anything different but slow down
I hold a little more awareness
To the space my mind requires
Before marbles are lost and I'm out here crossing wires
Burned out, I may be stuck in the sunken place
With no lights but much fight
The world on my side
I shall find elevation through desire

Herb Seeker

Seek out ye who finds peace, with the herb
Seek the company of ye who makes tea, with the herb
For they are peaceful and wise
Seek out ye who can provide you with fresh dry cured herbs
They are commonly sought in the market place
Beware of touts
And con men in the market are commonplace
Seek you a trusted source
Men and Women worthy of your hard earned
Ground, cooked, boiled or burned
Man has found many a use for the herb

The o116

Hear the dialect strewn through the fabric of my cit
If you're like me then you might b
A stones throw from brok
A pocket full of le
Swanky with the dress but still got now
Nup'n
But it's all good chic
As long as I have oxygen, money ain't shi
Water off a ducks back to the lack of i
We step with pride past the shire
With not a shrapnel in our pocket
& what's there to be mardy about
Children stay ramping, hand clappin
Grateful when the sun is ou
We send mardy arse to the shop
With clear instructio
Don't return with less than fruit salads, black jacks and two sacks of penny sweet
That was back in the day, I'm talking Larch stree
Today, we still send a mardy arse to the sho
With a different set of need

Bring me rizzla, skittles, a magnum and a 30 pence tip top
Just like quintessentially British weather
Leicester doesn't really change much
With the familiarity of a good pair of hand me downs
The city remains a bastion of love
Bop through any jitty without fear of being rushed
Long before playgrounds became shit
Before kids became addicted to candy crush
We worshipped the grass hill
The sacred location where games required skill
Hot rice, British Bull Dog, knock-a-door-run
Fox and hounds, track down, every Saturday blood had to spill
Before any tears came
I would hear mum call my name
'Dinner time!'
So I would go hold my fill
Something hearty and stodgey
Food digested, I'm back outta street moving froggy
This was when the real MVP was dishing out croggeys
It sounds like I'm growin' into an old fart, probably
I'm a child of Leicester
I could care less about celebrity
Because in Lesta, we take care of our own!
I know my city will remember me and Lesta will always be home!

New Home

This land does not feel like home, yet
This earth between my toes is not the sand I'm accustomed to
The customs too
Are alien
Few and far between do people dance in the street
Waving arms in celebration
Dancing with spirit
Oozing public joy profusely
Loosely does this place imitate the image sold through the news
Beemed across the interweb to entrap the hearts and minds of me and you
Consumer protection is just a word and I'm confused
This is not the dream I purchased
My ticket was sold with front row seats to opportunity
Whereas in practice I'm so bogged down
I rarely see the surface
For this life I left family
Some write to me, some call
Some call me crazy
Just lately, I see what they mean
Sour sop, ugli fruit and bammy
Has been replaced with occasional fruit bun
And patties that will never see flaky pastry
I reiterate
This land does not feel like home, yet
I have travelled great distances to be here
I might not be here for ever
Might not be here for long
Whilst I am here
I'm bringing culture, vibes, food, great moods
Poetry, reasoning, seasoning, spiritual greetings
And I'm bringing it strong!
This place does not feel like home yet
A little sugar an' a little colour an' it wont be long!

Banana Juice

I love you like the fat kid loves cake
I love you like the gazelle loves the chase
I love you, more than you love banana juice
If that's not true
I'll kidnap all your favourite Disney princesses
And for good measure I'm bringing Baloo
To the stirchley baths
Where we'll have a laugh
And throw a party just for you
Because if I don't love you
More than you love Banana juice
I'm taking all the magical people you knew
Into exile
Where we'll dine together at the end of the rainbow over heartbreak stew
For any who claim this love is not true is a liar
And a thief
They would rather you cement over the cracks
Than step back to admire the crack from which the rose grew
Delicate yet mighty
It is the love within the rose that truly encourages the earth to move
I'll be your Tramp if you be my Lady
Brian to your Snow White
Eric to your Ariel
I love you like mad and I'm willing to die crazy
I love you more than you love banana juice my lady

Constant

Icy peaks cast long shadows over the parched earth
Vegetation is sparse and brittle
Browse the riverbeds
Find no worth in the baron grandscape
The remnants of death are ever present
The memory of life in this place is evanescent
Cramped between the endless needs of two worlds
This has become the baron land
Within its grotesquely picturesque frame
Manifests unfulfilled dreams
A petri dish for misspent intention
Unspent attention finds its way here
Seeps into earth's pores
Sucking all remaining life from between the toes of the land
It is dry here, the air is arid
Laden with scorched earth brushed, swept even
Across a mute canvas
On the back of a wind free to shape the landscape in a bluster of madness
The sun does not set here
At its worst, all the flaws of this place are clear
When the eye is sodden with desolation
It is translucent as to why the end is here is met with impatience
Love is of no relation to the process of death and creation
There are places in this world of unimaginable beauty
Unsafe for us to visit
But the rift between two people
Inevitable in the coming together of two worlds
Pangea itself isn't a perfect fit
Must be observed and nurtured by taking care of the world around it
Love is not free from conflict
But between you and me
May it be love that remains the constant eternally

Teary Estuary

Priceless are the eyes that have seen hope when all else
fades
Lakes of sorrow swell anticlockwise
Fed my a nation of cry babies perched dockside
It is difficult to maintain buoyancy
When the tide directly collides
With every stride taken forward
Despite the fact we suffer collectively
It will take more than one to lead the herd to the estuary
Where the open sea and teary streams
Swill to form brackish water
Our thirst for better means we drink
Our immediate dismay means we drink
Even though we know this is brine
Which may make our lives considerably shorter
We either keep swimming upstream
Drown in this sorrow like a lamb to the slaughter
Or face the open sea with no dingy borrowed

A Beauty Lost

If beauty does loose its way
I pray it should greet you at the end of your tether
Whether peace should stay your way
Is a matter of measure and perspective
I can only pray beauty awaits your ready heart and steady mind
This labyrinth will lead you down dead ends many a time
Gut wrenching failure always seems to keep you ten steps from your prime
Ambition is an expensive game
A pocket full of lint won't get you far I'm afraid
Money helps
But it's a whole different metric when you're trying to escape
Whatever subplots and twists your journey may contain
I pray that at the end of your tether
Beauty should find its place
Your adventure deserves to finish in the most wonderful of states
Complain, but that's just not how it always goes
So on the quest to experience life's true gold
When the trail goes cold
No one understands
And you can't help but feel alone
I pray you see beauty
And it stares you boldly in the face
Long enough for you to pucker up
Give thanks, and be on your way

I Too Shall Miss You

I am going to cry when you're gone
I will not cry when I see you leave
I will cry when you're gone
I probably won't tell you every time I cry
So I, am telling you now
I will cry at the thought of you
I will clutch at your thighs only to arrive at an empty sarong
Nuttun wrong except an inability to nestle my head
In-between the space between your breast
I will cry when you're gone
Seeking comfort in your scent
As distance relents
I find strength in knowing I'm coming to you
Yes I will cry when you're gone
But it will be temporary
Love based on distance may be stretched
With the love we posses
No distance it too long
Don't worry about my crying in your absence
Join me in looking forward to
Reuniting over foreign food
Black sand beaches and the naked sun

Word Power

Powers
A grain of sand for every hour
And you and everybody you know wouldn't amount to a pleasure
beach In the east part of Glasgow
The power of words lies in their faceless value
I can articulate things that couldn't possibly be as beautiful
As I've made out in stanza and verse
More times than not, true is the inverse
Not always but a multitude of times I have pick pocketed
The minds and mouths of listeners
So I may fill my own purse
And there is no offering at this church
This church I have built for myself
My own reality with no chapel
Nor windows for dreams nor mirrors for vanity
You will find no one sacrificing their charity
No sermon poised as divine
Or even containing any clarity
What you will find are words of encouragement
Words you do not want to hear
Words you didn't know you didn't want to hear
Words to heal

Words to expose
Words to conceal
Words that burn a mighty hole in those they touch
Words that unite
And characters that corrupt
The only thing I offer or present as valuable;
Is dialogue
Are words
If you should wish to build or destroy
Words must be employed
Articulate, create
Never argue though always be up for debate
These little buggars of mine
Used every day, by us all
Are the reason we have gods
All the same reason nations will fall
Use them wisely
Or do me the courtesy of not using them at all

Florilegium

Florilegium

Boston 'The Orator' Williams